Finger rings

from ancient to modern

Diana Scarisbrick and
Martin Henig
with an introduction by
James Fenton

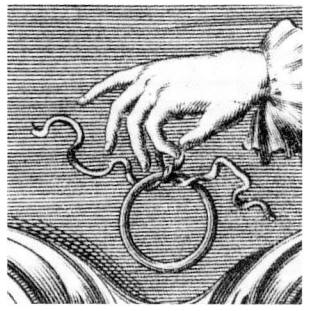

Published with the aid of a
generous grant
from Benjamin Zucker

Ashmolean Museum Oxford
2003

ISBN 1 85444 166 3 (paperback)
ISBN 1 85444 167 1 (papercased)

Titles in this series include:
The Ashmolean Museum
Drawings by Michelangelo and Raphael
Ruskin's drawings
Samuel Palmer
J.M.W. Turner
Camille Pissarro and his family
French drawings and watercolours
Oxford and the Pre-Raphaelites
Twentieth century paintings
Miniatures
English Delftware
Worcester porcelain
Eighteenth-century French porcelain
Maiolica
Islamic ceramics
Indian paintings from Oxford collections
Ancient Greek pottery
Scythian and Thracian treasures
Frames and framings

British Library Cataloguing in Publication Data
A catalogue record for this book is available from the British
Library

Title page illustration: Trade card of Elizabeth Godfrey, jeweller at
the Hand, Ring and Crown, Norris Street, St.James's, Haymarket,
c.1750
Cover illustration: Thame reliquary ring, plate 11

Designed and typeset in Versailles by Roy Cole, Wells
Printed and bound in Singapore by Craft Print International Ltd

It gives me great pleasure to be sponsoring this book as my friendship with the author, Diana Scarisbrick, is founded on our passion for jewellery, and rings in particular. We first met in 1976 when we were both looking at the Fortnum Collection in the Ashmolean Museum, and ever since we have collaborated most happily together.

Benjamin Zucker

The author would like to express her gratitude to Mr Zucker for his enthusiastic support, and also to Jennifer Marin of the Jewish Museum, London, who kindly assisted her research.
The photography was undertaken by Bob Wilkins in Oxford University's Institute of Archaeology and by the Ashmolean Museum's own photographers. Additional photographs for comparative illustrations and monotone figures were supplied courtesy of the Bodleian Library, Oxford, the British Museum and the Cabinet des Estampes.

Collecting rings

One of the old authorities on rings describes how, when a Pope dies, the cardinal chamberlain or chancellor, accompanied by a large number of dignitaries of the papal court, enters the room where the body lies, and the principal notary makes an attestation of the circumstance. 'Then the cardinal chamberlain calls out the name of the deceased pope three times, striking the body each time with a gold hammer.' If the pope shows no sign of life the chief notary makes a further attestation. After this, the cardinal chancellor demands the Fisherman's Ring, [with which the popes sign their bulls and briefs] and certain ceremonies are performed over it; and then he strikes the ring with the golden hammer, and an officer destroys the figure of Peter by use of a file. From this moment all the authority and acts of the late pope pass to the College or Conclave of Cardinals. When a new pope is consecrated, it is always the cardinal chancellor who presents the renewed Fisherman's Ring; and this presentation is accompanied by imposing ceremonies.[1]

One can hardly think of a better illustration of the ancient power and significance of the ring, for we see that the Fisherman's Ring has a legal force in and of itself. As soon as its owner dies, it must be rendered useless. One cannot allow a situation to arise whereby there are old Fisherman's Rings that might fall into the wrong hands or get placed on the wrong fingers, or back-dated bulls and briefs start flying around all over the place. The officer takes his file and destroys (the act almost seems blasphemous) the figure of Peter, the fisher of men. Now the ring has lost its power. The Barclaycard has been cut in two, and the PIN number cancelled.

[1] The History and Poetry of Finger-Rings by Charles Edwards, New York 1855 pp.77–8.

Actually, in societies where rings had legal status, to lose your signet ring was far worse than losing your credit cards: to lose your ring was to lose your signature. In Persia, the same curious book further informs us, as recently as the nineteenth century, letters were seldom written and never signed by the person who sent them. The authenticity of the letter – even of something so commonplace as a merchant's bill – depended entirely upon the impression of the seal ring. So we are told that the occupation of the seal-cutter was one of as much trust and danger in Persia as it seems to have been in ancient Egypt. The seal-cutter was obliged to keep a register of every ring seal he made, and if one was lost or stolen from the party for whom it was cut, his life would answer for making another exactly like it.

And just as the expiry date on a credit card has become a means of authenticating a transaction, so the date of cutting might be important on a seal. If you lost your seal ring, and you suspected that someone was intending to use it rather than simply melt it down, the only thing to do was to have another seal made with a new date, and to write to all your correspondents to inform them that all accounts, contracts and communications to which your former signet is affixed are null from the day on which it was lost.

This business about seals reminds us why rings are so important, and why they figure so prominently in history and legend. Of all cultural objects represented in a museum such as the Ashmolean, they have changed least over the millennia. A ring, in essence, has one, two or three elements. The circle, which is called the hoop or shank. The *bezel*, which is the part where the seal or the gem is placed. And then on some rings there is a transitional area between the hoop and the *bezel*, and that is called the shoulders. Once you know these three terms – the hoop, the *bezel* and the shoulders – you are well on the way to becoming your own ring expert.

Now even though the ring is perfectly simple, its significance may be immense: the modern wedding ring, a plain gold hoop, may be the wearer's most valued possession. Imagine though the significance of a gold ring in a society where not everybody is allowed to wear one. Rings from the ancient Near East are, we are told, extremely rare and amongst the first group illustrated here on page 17 is the finest of all Hittite signet rings. It dates from 1400–1300 BC.

At the centre of the signet is a god above a sphinx between two lions, the symbols, we are told, for Great and Prince. You don't have to be Sherlock Holmes to come to the conclusion that this is the seal of a great Hittite prince, that it was his identifying possession: his signature, his fingerprint, his credit card number with his expiry date, his passport, his driver's license, his DNA – whatever you will. And it would have been known to his subjects, through its imprint on clay tablets. It would have been, as it were, a famous and venerated object, unique to its owner.

Often, in history and in legend or fiction, a story turns upon the fact that a ring or jewel is recognised as belonging to someone important. And it is true that rings were known and recognised and that the passing of a ring from one person to another could have an awesome significance. When pharaoh in the legend took the ring from his hand and gave it to Joseph, that meant that Joseph was now governor of all Egypt. Anyone who saw the ring on Joseph's hand would know what it signified.

This recognition of rings is much more likely in a society in which not everybody is entitled to wear them. Obviously there is not much recognition factor in a world in which all married women wear wedding rings – the wedding ring is like a uniform. But at various periods in, for instance, the history of ancient Rome, the wearing of gold rings was restricted to certain classes. We are told that knights, in ancient Rome, were entitled to three perks: a charger provided at the state's expense, the right to wear a

6

gold ring, and thirdly – their own seat at the theatre.

Plutarch, in his gruesome life of Caius Marius, the Roman consul, tells us how Marius as a young officer went to Africa to make his career in the war against Jugurtha, the king of Numidia. Such was his popularity with the army, he was elected consul, and went back to Africa with one plan in mind: to capture Jugurtha and bring him back in chains. Unfortunately his rival Sulla managed to pip him to the post, and captured Jugurtha through a cunning act of treachery. Whereupon Sulla had a ring engraved. On the seal, there was depicted the King Jugurtha surrendering to Sulla. From Marius's point of view this was outrageous: if Jugurtha had surrendered, technically speaking he was the boss, and Sulla had no right to have such a ring made. So this ring had tremendous consequences in the history of Rome. It was the cause of the fierce hatred between Marius and Sulla.

So we find that rings were, like the Pope's Fisherman's ring, or Pharaoh's ring, or the Doge's ring (which he had to surrender on being deposed) actual instruments of power, or powerful symbols of authority. They could identify an individual, or a member of a class. It is not surprising to find that rings were also, from an early age, credited with powers of their own.

Charles Oman, in his books on British rings, tells the following story. In 1538 Sir Edward Neville, an expert on astrology, received a summons from William Neville to visit him in Oxford. He arrived and was taken into a little room and asked whether it was possible 'to have a ring made that should bring a man to favour with his prince; seeing that my Lord Cardinal [Wolsey] had such a ring that whatsoever he asked of the King's Grace, that he had.'[2] And William Neville also believed that Thomas Cromwell had such a ring, which made him powerful with Cardinal Wolsey. One famous thing about Wolsey was, of course, that he was a butcher's son. His possession of a ring would explain his rise to power. Another source informs us that

[2]British Rings, 800–1914 by Charles Oman, London 1974 p.59.

Thomas Cromwell was believed to possess King Solomon's ring.

Rings were credited with religious powers, with magical properties and with medical virtues, but it is impossible to draw a clear distinction between these three, since the wearers and makers of these rings made no clear distinction themselves. When St. Thomas Aquinas was asked about the use of inscribed charms he said that they were only permissible if no evil spirits were therein invoked, no incomprehensible words used, no deceit or belief in any other power than the power of God, no character used other than the sign of the Cross, and no faith placed in the manner of the inscription.

However it very often happens that rings are found with biblical inscriptions which are in fact charms. *Consummatum est,* 'It is finished', Christ's last words on the cross, became a charm to calm storms. *Iesus autem transiens per medium illorum ibat* – 'But Jesus passed through the middle of them and went away' [Luke 4.30], a line describing Jesus's escape from the enraged crowd in Nazareth who wished to throw him off a cliff, became a charm against thieves. Sir John Mandeville says that people pronounce these words 'when thei dreden them of thefes on any way, or of enemyes, in token and mynde that our Lord passed through out of the Jews' crueltie and scaped safely fro hem.'[3]

Put like that, one might say that Aquinas would have no objection to the use of such a text on a ring, but the fact is that is was not simply that travellers, when in danger, meditated on the dangers that Christ had gone through. They also believed that the wearing of such a ring would make one invisible. Edward the Third had issued a coin, a noble, with the same text, and people had come to believe that the text conferred immunity 'against both theft of the coin and harm to its owner'. Queen Elizabeth sent one of these coins to the Earl of Essex to guard him on the 1597 expedition to the Azores. A ring which was believed to have belonged to the Black Prince bore the same

[3] Cited in Rings for the Finger by George Frederick Kunz , Philadelphia 1917 (Dover Edition reprint) p.315.

inscription, followed by the words Et Verbum C – an incomplete version of the phrase *Et Verbum Caro Factum Est* – and the word was made flesh, another phrase used as a charm on rings.

Now one of the things that Aquinas said was that no incomprehensible words should be used, and that was because the use of incomprehensible words – as in *abracadabra* or *hocus pocus* – was characteristic of magical charms rather than religious ritual properly so conceived. But it would undoubtedly have been the case that these phrases like *Consummatum Est* were used by people who had no idea of their meaning, only a sense of their power. A ring in the Ashmolean is inscribed with the words *Caspar, Melchior, Balthasar* – the three kings. These names were said to protect against epilepsy. One invoked the three kings, the twelve apostles, and the four evangelists in a powerful charm that also used incomprehensible words, or words chosen for their power rather than their meaning as such. Tetragrammaton, a word referring to the four Hebrew letters in God's name, occurs on rings, as does *Ananizapta* (a word made out of the initials of a formula for curing epilepsy), which had the added usefulness of protecting one against drunkenness. *BURO + BERTO + BERNETO* is a charm against toothache. It is nonsense. *GVGVE-CEUBEAVALDERA VRVA IALRRA PHAECARAO* is complete and utter gibberish as is *Gut Got hunuyu ananizapta*.

The reason why Aquinas, as we have seen, disapproved of gibberish on rings was that it implied an appeal to an improper source of power. Now if we think of, for instance, a ring with an image of St Christopher, and we say: the meaning of this ring is that this saint will intercede on behalf of travellers, so this is a religious ring, not a magical one – we might be quite wrong. The meaning of the ring could equally be that he who gazes on an image of Saint Christopher is thereby protected from sudden death. Such a ring would therefore be potentially both religious and magical.

9

The ring illustrated in Plate 11, which is part of the Thame hoard, found in 1940, is one of the grandest rings in the Ashmolean and one of the great surviving pieces of medieval jewelry. It is of French work, from the late fourteenth century, probably made either in Paris or by a French goldsmith working for Richard II. The whole of the *bezel* can be dismantled, and the back of the *bezel* has on one side a leafy design, while the crucifixion scene would be in contact with the skin of the owner.

We ask ourselves how it fulfills the criteria laid down by Aquinas. No evil spirits seem to be invoked. Apart from the misspelt Memanto, no incomprehensible words are used. The third criterion was No Deceit. And that depends on whether you believe that it could have contained a piece of the True Cross, as it purported to do. No characters used other than the sign of the cross – one could debate that, since the Cross of Lorraine was probably not what Aquinas had in mind. The last criterion was that no faith be placed in the manner of the inscription, but I think that this placing of the hidden crucifixion scene against the skin would be exactly the sort of practice that would have counted as superstition.

This would have been the ring of a very important bishop or other church figure. One reason why so little of such jewelry survives is that, if it had been in a church treasury it would have been confiscated at the Reformation. Some bishops' rings survived because they were buried with their owners, but rings in general were not collected and preserved always for generation after generation. They were not thought of as objects of antiquarian interest until, of course, antiquarianism came along.

By antiquarianism we mean a kind of inquiry into the past that has its origins in the seventeenth century, when the first books about old rings were written, and when people like the Tradescants and Elias Ashmole himself made their collections of curiosities, which were the basis of the original Ashmolean Museum. Antiquarianism was the precursor of archaeology and various kinds of historical research, as well as connoisseurship of the modern kind. The great connoisseur Horace Walpole had a small collection of rings on display at Strawberry Hill, in the following century.

I recently bought a catalogue of a ring collection given to a German museum. The catalogue was very handsome and the museum had obviously been thrilled to receive the collection: it contained thirty ancient rings. And indeed thirty rings is definitely a good collection. The bulk of the Ashmolean's collection comes from Charles Drury Fortnum. That nucleus consists of 800 rings, but when a full catalogue was made in1978 it listed over a thousand.

Fortnum was a man with a happy knack for marrying wealthy wives, and he spent much time on the continent building up his collections, particularly in Venice and Rome. Several of the early ecclesiastical rings Fortnum was lucky to acquire were from Murano, where they must have been buried with clergy of high rank. Others came from a Venetian fort in Greece, as part of the celebrated Chalcis hoard, which contained not only rings but also some highly unusual early medieval armour.

Fortnum had been keen that his collections should be kept together so that the old Ashmolean would develop 'into an institution of the first importance for teaching and illustrating the development of art as applied to both small and larger objects.' However, the division of the museum's collections between antiquities and western art means that the ring collection has been dispersed among different rooms. Of course it is still there, it is just not as obvious to the visitor that he is in the presence of a great collection of rings – the greatest in this country after those in the Victoria and Albert and the British Museum.

Although it would be hard to imagine anyone, however wealthy, building up a collection of antique rings to rival the Ashmolean's, it is perfectly conceivable that a quite modest collector could put together a group of rings which future generations would admire just as much as we admire these rings. After all, what Fortnum was collecting was not highly or widely prized in his day. Jewelry goes out of fashion, becomes disprized, is melted down and its stones get recycled. Types of rings have become rare because they have passed through this kind of phase of unpopularity.

As mentioned above, ancient rings are still found. Although there seem to be no shops left in London that specialise in such objects, there are a few which feature unusual antique jewelry as a side-line. The auction rooms will include interesting old rings, from time to time, in their sales of European Works of Art. Beyond such establishments, the whole thing is partly a matter of luck, partly a question of knowledge, judgment, perseverance. Knowledge starts with the objects themselves: the three greatest British public collections have already been mentioned – the British Museum, the Victoria and Albert Museum and the Ashmolean. The easiest ring-book to find is the Dover reprint of George Frederick Kunz's *Rings for the Finger*. Beautifully illustrated, and with a good introductory text, is Diana Scarisbrick's *Rings, Symbols of wealth, power and affection* (Thames and Hudson 1993). Charles Oman's *British Rings* (Batsford 1974) is another place to begin. After that it is a matter of following up references, and seeking out the scholarly catalogues of the important collections.

Of the numerous kinds of ring in existence, the least likely to turn up is a poison-ring such as Cesare Borgia was said to have owned. The curious old book from which I have quoted above, by Charles Edwards, tells us that the *bezel* of this ring was composed of two lion's heads, which Borgia would turn inwards before pressing the hand of someone he wished to kill: 'It was then the lion's teeth became those of a viper charged with poison.' But these Borgia poison rings appear, alas, to belong to legend.

James Fenton

Part 1: Rings in the ancient Mediterranean world

Rings were used throughout Antiquity, serving as jewellery, for use as seals, as keepsakes and as amulets and on occasion for several of these functions together. They are made in all metals and the preponderance of gold in the examples selected here is perhaps misleading; the aim was to present a good selection of the finer specimens; many rings were of silver, iron or bronze.

The Ashmolean is fortunate to contain a good selection of Near Eastern gems including Egyptian scarabs worn on swivel hoops and ancestral in form (though not in the subject matter of their devices) and scarab-rings of Archaic Greece and Etruscan Italy. Egyptian art influenced Cyprus as well as other cultures, including no doubt Hittite Anatolia. The Ashmolean's ring is in fact the finest Hittite ring still extant. One of the Etruscan rings shown is also Egyptianising in the arrangement of its motifs and perhaps in the device itself which seems to be Nilotic and includes water birds, ichneumon and cobra.

Even more important is the very large collection of Cretan seals in the collection, mainly assembled by Sir Arthur Evans, including a superb stone ring. The theme of wild goats pulling a chariot shows the subject matter is religious and has to do with cult rather than with everyday life. Until very recently the two gold rings (one from the Greek mainland) assigned to the Thisbe group, named after a site in Crete, shown here were rejected as spurious but tests have now shown them to be genuine and very important late Bronze Age antiquities.

The Greeks, as stated above, began by using gems shaped as scarabs set in swivel hoops; illustrated here is an Etruscan gem close to the Greek

Archaic style and itself dating to the sixth century. By Classical times Greek gem rings contain scaraboids (with the backs no longer carved as beetles) and the museum has a fair number of these, cut with devices that display the new virtuosity and naturalism of fifth century Greek art. The same concerns are displayed on all-metal rings. One of these illustrated here depicts a portrait (or near portrait) of a man, quite close to a famous gem in Boston by the famous gem-cutter Dexamenos. True portraiture only begins in the Hellenistic period as represented by the portrait of the Ptolemaic queen Berenike I, on a gold *bezel* set on an iron ring. The Etruscans of the classical period continued to be very much influenced by Greek Art. Especially close to classical models is a ring depicting Herakles relaxing, a type looking forward to the work of Lysippos in the fourth century but probably earlier. It is thus tempting to consider it with truly classical works.

A Greek ring, rather later than either of these, has a charming inconsequentiality looking towards the Hellenistic age. It shows Eros with a torch and was perhaps a love token. Eros was said to have singed the wings of Psyche with a torch, symbolising the violence that the body perpetrates on the soul. Here the allusion is to the punishment of Eros for his crime. An early Roman ring depicting a satyr in *intaglio* really belongs to the end of the Hellenistic age and is a happy evocation of the symposium (drinking party).

By no means all rings were figural. An extraordinary silver ring displays a man's name in relief; clearly not a seal – perhaps it was a pass to allow the owner entrance to some building or sanctuary. A final Greek ring-type represented here, the serpent ring, is certainly symbolic and of a type which continued to be popular in the Roman period and was adapted in highly distinctive ways elsewhere. Larger versions were used as bracelets or even worn (by prostitutes) on the thigh, so ubiquitous were these life-giving images.

Although the Romans took their use of rings

from the Etruscans and the Greeks, rings came to assume especial significance as badges of rank. The gold ring was originally the preserve of senators and especially members of the Equestrian order ('knights'). We know from a number of writers that, however wealthy they were, freedmen (people not of free birth) were forbidden to wear gold rings and were forced to wear iron ones, which they nevertheless embellished with gilding like the notorious parvenu Trimalchio, who figures in Petronius' novel *The Satyricon*. Later such strict sumptuary laws were relaxed and Septimius Severus, for instance, allowed all soldiers to wear the gold ring.

Early Roman rings had simple circular or ribbon hoops often set with an exquisite gem in the *bezel* in the fashion of Hellenistic times. By the second century rings were becoming more showy with wide hoops or, in the case of a ring shown here with wine-vessels and lyres depicted on the hoop, intricately fashioned. Gems such as the emerald, here set so that the light can shine through it, were first imported from the East after Alexander the Great's campaigns but the use of such rare and exotic stones as ring settings perhaps becomes commoner from Roman times. Roman rings reach their apogee of sophistication in the third and fourth centuries; devices became less important and a fine, expensive gold ring in the collection has a very pedestrian cornelian setting. Sometimes the quality of the stone was what counted and it remained unengraved. A superb example of this is a sapphire-set ring which seems to have been a gift, perhaps a love token, to a Greek (man?) called Olympis. It was found early in the nineteenth century in Suffolk and presumably belonged to a Greek-speaking immigrant. It is certainly not only perhaps the finest Roman ring in the Museum, but amongst the best from Roman Britain. The only real rivals are a group of gold rings from later in the fourth century found at Thetford in Norfolk, and now in the British Museum.

Martin Henig

Plate 1

Egyptian and Near Eastern rings

1   Gold swivel-ring containing a *faience* scarab with on the underside in *intaglio* a lotus flower device. The ring dates to the period of the New Kingdom (1550–1070 B.C.) and is said to have been found at Thebes in Egypt. *Bezel*: 11 × 14; Hoop D.: 22.
AN Fortnum R5

2   Gold ring with wide *bezel* showing in *intaglio* a winged Hittite god above a sphinx, flanked by two lions as symbols of his power. This is the finest of all Hittite signet rings and was bought at Konya by W.M.Ramsay. Hoop D.: 28·5.
AN 1896-1908 O. 6

3   Gold ring with massive solid hoop cut with an ovoid *intaglio* showing the god Ptah enthroned with the winged sun disc above two *ankhs* with a T-shaped symbol between. The ring is Cypriot, Egyptianising work, probably found at Enkomi in Cyprus. *Bezel*: 19 × 17; Hoop D.: 17.
AN 1962.242

1

2

3

17

Plate 2

Aegean rings

1   Agate ring. The stone is slightly leached and the hoop is broken. The convex, oval *bezel* show two men in a chariot drawn by a pair of *agrimi* (Cretan wild goats). The ring was found at Avdou near Lyttos, and dates from the period when Minoan Crete was evidently ruled by a mainland, Mycenaean dynasty (1450–1300 B.C.). *Bezel*: 23 × 28; Hoop D.: 23.
AN 1938.1051

2   Gold ring with broad hoop, embellished with a row of pellets between beading. The ovoid field is divided into four zones by broad irregular channels which could represent river channels. In the upper left two votaries kneel in front of a plinth upon which is a recumbent lion. In the lower left are a woman in a flared skirt (the goddess), a griffin on a pedestal and three other figures. In the upper right are four figures, two standing, one kneeling and one seated; in the lower right four figures. Clearly these are cult scenes. This ring, belonging to the 'Thisbe' group (named for a site in Bolona) was called by Sir Arthur Evans, the 'Ring of Nestor' as it was found at Kakovatos (Pylos), the site of Nestor's palace, in the Peloponnese. (*c*.1500–1300 B.C.). *Bezel*: 35 × 22; Hoop D.: 25.
AN 1938.1130

3   Gold ring with broad hoop, ornamented with four channels between five rows of beading. The device on the ovoid *bezel* is the well-known Cretan theme of an acrobat leaping on the back of a bull. The ring comes from Archanes near Knossos, Crete. (*c*.1450–1300 B.C.). *Bezel*: 35 × 23; Hoop D.: 22.
AN Ae.2237

1

2

3

Plate 3

Greek rings

1   Gold ring with simple hoop, circular in section, and leaf-shaped *bezel*. It bears in *intaglio* the bearded head of a middle-aged man with sharp pointed nose and heavy brows. The interest in character here marks an important advance in the development of portraiture. East Greek. From a grave at Nymphaeum (Tumulus IV) in the Crimaea. Third quarter of the fifth century B.C. *Bezel*: 15 × 10; Hoop D.: 22.
AN 1885.484

2   Gold ring with wide ribbon hoop and circular *bezel*, with the *intaglio* device of Eros standing and facing a torch which appears to be falling away from him; perhaps he has burnt himself. From Athens. Late fourth· or early third century B.C. *Bezel*: 20 × 21; Hoop D.: 20.
AN Fortnum R.117

3   Silver ring with flat ribbon hoop and circular *bezel* with in relief applied gilt Greek letters ΞΕΝΟΔΟΚΑΣ (Xenodokas), fourth century B.C. *Bezel*: 25 × 25; Hoop D.: 20.
AN 1921.864

4   Serpent ring of gold. A gold ring in the form of a snake, the body in two coils serving as a double loop. Scales are shown naturalistically running down the full length of the creature. Snakes, which slough their skins frequently, were potent symbols of life in the Graeco-Roman world. This is said to come from Ptolemaic Egypt. Third–first century B.C. *Bezel*: 14 × 17; Hoop D.: 21.
AN 1873.122j

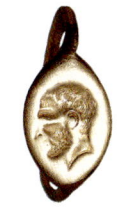

1

2

3

4

Plate 4

Etruscan rings

1   Gold ring with cartouche containing three regis-
ters, above a bird and branch; in the middle a seated figure with a branch behind him, an ichneumon
(mongoose), a long legged water bird and a serpent
(cobra?); a bird and two other creatures below. This is
Egyptianising work, in part having a Nilotic theme, of
the sixth century. *Bezel* W.: 23; H.: 11. Hoop D.: 22.
AN Fortnum R.763

2   Gold ring with solid hoop and cup shaped ends; a
swivel hoop containing a scarab in agate with, on the
underside, an *intaglio* depicting a youth holding a neck-
lace within a beaded border. The work is quite close to
archaic Greek gem-cutting in style (by the 'Master of the
Boston Dionysos'). The ring, bought in Rome, is said to
have been found in Tarquinia. Late sixth century B.C.
Bezel: 7 × 9; Hoop D.: 22.
AN Fortnum R.74

3   Gold ring with ribbon hoop and pointed ovoid
bezel. Within a beaded border is shown in relief the
young Herakles seated upon his lion skin. He holds his
club in his right hand, and seeks to rest his chin against
its upper end. He grasps his right knee in his left hand.
From Praeneste. Second half of fifth century B.C. *Bezel*:
19 × 25; Hoop D.: 29.
AN Fortnum R.85

1

2

3

Plate 5

Roman rings

1   Gold ring with hoop in the form of a pair of can-
thari with a lyre above each. The square *bezel* has an
open back in order to allow light to pass through an
emerald cut with the portrait of the Empress Faustina II
(A.D. 161–176), wife of Marcus Aurelius. *Bezel*: 19 × 17;
Hoop D.: 17.
AN 1962.434

2   Heavy gold ring with *keeled* hoop and triangular
shoulders channelled to look like two sprays of acan-
thus. In the *bezel* is a raised cornelian *intaglio* depicting
an ant, the familiar of the corn-goddess, Ceres. Third
century A.D. *Bezel*: 15 × 11; Hoop D.: 28.
AN Fortnum R.176

3   Gold ring with *keeled* hoop and triangular shoulders with delicate leaf edging inscribed in Greek on one
shoulder, ΟΛΥΜΠΕΙ and on the other ΖΗΣΑΙΣ, '[Long]
life to Olympis'. There is a palm at the beginning and
another at the end of the inscription. The *bezel* is set
with a plain *cabochon* blue sapphire. Found in Stonham
Aspal, Suffolk in 1811. Third or early fourth century A.D.
Bezel: 6; Hoop.: 26.
AN 1933.1693

1

2

3

Part 2: Medieval and later rings

Medieval men and women of all classes wore gold, silver and gilt bronze rings, sometimes more than one on each finger and on both the upper and lower joints. Most were set with gems, prized for their beauty, rarity and the powers attributed to them by the lapidaries: the sapphire detected fraud and protected chastity, while the ruby, if rubbed into the four corners of a room, would make it safe from storms. These properties were reinforced by magical or Biblical inscriptions, also believed to heal and protect. The earliest designs were the simple stirrup shaped hoop rising to an apex, and the 'pie-dish' *bezel* enclosing the stone in a wide rim, joined to a plain hoop. The stones, 'en *cabochon*', were secured by claws, and in the case of the thirteenth-century sapphire rings from Murano, guarded by dragons at the shoulders. In contrast to these fierce watch dogs, sprigs of flowers, once bright with enamels, flank the six sided peridot in the oval cusped *bezel* of an English late fourteenth-century ring. The high point of Gothic elegance is attained by the rings found in 1840 in the Greek castle of Chalcis, 400 years after the capture of this prosperous Venetian colony by the Turks. Some have tall *bezels* lavishly mounted with pearls and rubies, and two flat *bezels* are set with a marcasite and a faceted sapphire. The courtly atmosphere of castle life is vividly evoked by a ring with *bezel* shaped as the rowel of a spur, and another like a miniature knight's belt of investiture. Some Chalcis signets bear the crests of the merchant families who exported a purple dye made from a local shell, others are set with rare Greek or Roman *intaglios*. Since seals were essential for all business transactions, those not entitled to bear arms used devices reflecting their personal interests, or, more usually, an initial. This being the age of faith, religion is the theme of an important category, splendidly exemplified by the ring from Thame containing a relic of the True Cross, belonging to a high ranking cleric. A distinctive English group, popular from the late fourteenth century until the Reformation, is engraved with devotional images – the Virgin and Child, the Trinity, patron saints – often combined on double or triple *bezels*. Each had a property of its own: St.Christopher, for instance who protected from sudden death, was the patron of travellers. Inscriptions indicate that these rings, named 'iconographic' by collectors, which were offered as gifts at New Year were also used at weddings as a less expensive alternative to diamond – in the natural point cut form – and pearl solitaires.

Belief that rings set with ass's hoof would cure epilepsy and that 'toadstones' – the fossilised teeth of fish – prevented dropsy continued strong well beyond the Renaissance. During that period however, great progress was made in faceting all stones, including the diamond which is now *table cut*. They are set in rings mirroring in miniature the art of the Italian Renaissance. Each part – *bezel*, shoulders, hoop – though clearly differentiated, merges into one harmonious composition. The most characteristic setting is the quatrefoil *bezel*, with 'shields' at the sides chased, and from the 1540s, enamelled. Larger stones are set in hexafoil, octofoil and box *bezels* similarly enriched. They are flanked by shoulders with *strapwork, volutes* or caryatids in high relief. Signets, of plain and simple design, placed conveniently on the thumb or index finger, were widely used. The most elaborate type was the *foiled crystal intaglio* with coat of arms engraved on crystal over foil painted with the colours, so that the arms stood out impressively on the hand. Each merchant had his own trademark or initialled version of the masted device which was painted over his shop and warehouses and stamped on bales of goods. The seventeenth- and eighteenth-century signet is rare, being superseded by seals in ornamental handles which hung from the watch chain.

There are several types of Renaissance love ring: the 'fede' with two hands clasped in love and trust, the Cupid cameo, and the dog, symbol of fidelity. Using the niello technique of the Florentine Maso Finiguerra (1426–1464) lovers are portrayed face to face on the bezels, and love mottoes are inscribed round the hoops of a group of Umbrian silver rings. The theme of marriage inspired the Renaissance goldsmith to create the 'gimmel' or twin ring with double bezel and hoops representing two lovers side by side, and this symbolism is further emphasised by an inscription affirming the indissolubility of the marriage vows. A particularly fine example incorporates ruby hearts and clasped hands with this inscription on the twin hoops. When closed up the twin parts fit together so well that the gimmel seems like just one, albeit important, ring. Jewish marriage rings are characterised by hoops with domed filigree bosses alternating with enamelled leaves and flowers, surmounted by a hinged bezel in the shape of a roof covering the Hebrew salutation MAZAL TOV, or Good Luck! The blue tiled roof symbolises either the couple's future home, or the Temple in Jerusalem. Whereas this type is well known, another, with canopied bezel similar to that under which the couple exchange their vows in the synagogue seems to be unique.

Symbols of death – skulls, cross-bones, hour glasses – warned of the brevity of life at a time of war, famine and plague. Sometimes the memento mori symbol is placed on one side of a swivel bezel, the reverse engraved for use as a seal. During the seventeenth century the memento mori ring with its stern symbolism developed into the memorial ring with name and date commemorating the death of a particular individual. The distribution of such rings to friends and relations remained part of the ritual of funerals until the last decades of the nineteenth century. The various changes of style over this long period which are exemplified by the Ashmolean collection culminate in the memorial ring to Victor Emmanuel II, King of Italy (1878).

The seventeenth-century wedding ring tells us much about contemporary attitudes to marriage. Plain gold hoops are inscribed with mottoes or 'posies', so called after the custom of offering flowers with a poem. Whether taken from printed books or specially composed for the occasion, posies, ranging from simple declarations of faithful love to humble prayers for God's blessing were always carefully chosen. Their solemnity contrasts with the more light hearted group of eighteenth-century love rings designed round the heart motif – single or twinned – aflame with passion, tied with a lover's knot or crowned. In France 'alliance' rings with two hearts, set with different stones, usually a diamond and a ruby, were used at weddings.

As for the decorative ring, there is a marked change in style around 1600, when the stone becomes the focus of design. Relief disappears from the shoulders, the hoop broadens and both are subordinated to the *bezel*, enamelled sober black and white. Since large diamonds were rare, the jewellers had to make the best of small stones, setting them in clusters of which the type with seven settings was almost standard. Quite different in spirit are the decorative rococo rings set with coloured stones in openwork bunches or vases of flowers, supported by forked shoulders, with a leaf filling the space between. Much larger in scale are the rings of the period after 1770 with elongated 'marquise' *bezels* whose weight is carried on hoops broadening at the shoulders.

Although the charm of rings lies in their personal associations, those which commemorate political events and famous individuals bring history to life. Most are portraits, but exceptionally, the ring of Thomas Gainsborough is set with moss agate with inclusions forming a landscape as beautiful as one painted by the artist himself.

Diana Scarisbrick

Plate 6

Medieval stone set rings

1   Gold stirrup ring with *cabochon* sapphire. Found at Canterbury. Thirteenth century. Hoop D.: 18 (263).

2   Gold ring with pie-dish *bezel* set with a *cabochon* ruby secured by claws. Found in Oxford. Thirteenth century. Hoop D.: 18 (252).

3   Silver ring with sapphire set in an hexagonal cusped raised *bezel* guarded by dragons at the shoulders. North Italian, fourteenth century. Hoop D.: 21 (3).

4   Silver ring with sapphire secured by claws in oval pie dish, *bezel*, guarded by dragons at the shoulders. North Italian, fourteenth century. Hoop D.: 18 (2).

5   Gold ring with hexagonal cusped *bezel* set with a peridot, flanked by flowers (formerly enamelled) at the shoulders. From Thame, fourteenth century. Hoop D.: 22 (AN 1940.227).

The austere settings of the early medieval rings are adapted to the shape of the *cabochon* stones, secured by claws. By the late fourteenth century, as the peridot ring shows, the claws have developed into cusping flanked by brightly coloured flowers which add to the decorative effect.

1

2

3   4   5

Plate 7

Decorative Veneto-Byzantine rings from the Chalcis hoard

1   Gold ring with a) high *bezel* pinned with six pearls guarded by flattened dragons at the shoulders; b) view of *niello* ornament on hoop. Late fourteenth, first half fifteenth century. Hoop D.: 20 (10).

2   Gold ring with *bezel* set with two oval garnets and two pearls, supported by hoop *nielloed* with lozenges between three rosettes. Hoop D.: 19 (13).

3   Gold ring with a) high inverted pyramidal *bezel* set with *cabochon* ruby, supported by hoop *nielloed* with scrolls; b) view of shoulders with dragons holding brackets and sides of *bezel* each *nielloed* with a flower. Hoop D.: 18 (11).

Threatened by invasion from the Turks in 1470, the rich Venetian inhabitants of Chalcis on the Greek island of Euboea hid their rings and other valuables in the castle. The discovery of the hoard in 1840 brought to light Gothic designs of a luxury and elegance surviving nowhere else.

Fig. 1
J.Scherrer, View of the castle at Chalcis, watercolour, 1854. Benaki Museum, Athens.

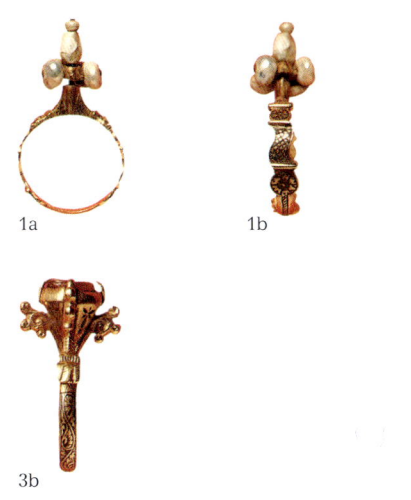

1a

1b

2

3a

3b

Plate 8

Decorative Veneto-Byzantine rings from Chalcis, continued

1   Gold ring with a) octagonal *bezel* set with *table cut* sapphire b) the openwork hoop formerly enamelled, interspersed with three Hercules knots each enclosing a star between line of pellets. Hoop D.: 18 (16).

2   Gold ring with octagonal pie dish *bezel* set with marcasite, supported by hoop terminating in lion's head shoulders. Hoop D.: 18 (17).

3   Gold ring with *bezel* in form of a spur with 12 pointed rowel held up by dragon heads at the shoulders on hoop with *nielloed* scrolls. Hoop D.: 17 (25).

4   Gold hollow hoop comprising four large (one missing) and four small panels inscribed in *black letter* VIRE VOS VOI between ALOL , a miniature version of a knight's belt. Hoop D.: 19 (22).

Contemporaries compared the round of balls and tournaments at Chalcis with the court of King Arthur at Avalon. Certainly, the knightly culture of chivalry, the excitement of the jousts in the castle courtyard, in the presence of beautifully attired women is evoked by the belt and spur rings, and by the fine quality of the others.

1a

1b

2

3

4

Plate 9

Veneto-Byzantine signets from Chalcis

1   Gold signet a) with round *bezel* engraved with an eagle within Greek inscription translating 'When you have enjoyed the world then you come to the tomb, Gold comes from the Clay Flesh from dust I have experienced both'; b) shoulders with roundels enclosing a lion, and an eagle with foliate decoration, fourteenth–fifteenth century. Hoop D.: 19 (19).

2   Gold signet a) with tall *bezel* set with amethyst *intaglio* of Fortuna (second century B.C.); b) view of hoop with Latin inscription in Lombardic letters ET VERBUM CARO FACTUM EST ET translating, 'and the Word was made Flesh and dwelt among us' (St. John I, v. 14). Hoop D.: 18 (12).

3   Gold signet with octagonal *bezel* engraved with crest of a Venetian nobleman, an eagle on helm, dragons *nielloed* on shoulders. Hoop D.: 19 (20).

Those involved in the trade which made Chalcis so rich used these signets to seal all business transactions, and at the same time were reminded that there was more to life than money making by the spiritual messages inscribed on them. The merging of the twin worlds of Byzantium and Venice in the colony is reflected in the ring with Greek inscription and Imperial eagle, and in the two others with Venetian heraldry and Latin quotation from the Gospel of St. John.

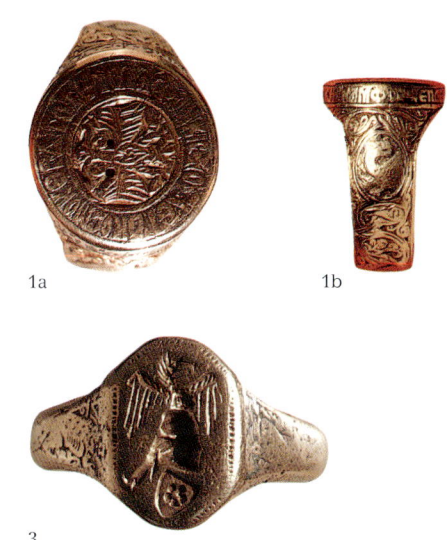

1a 1b

2a 2b 3

Plate 10

Other medieval signets

1   Silver signet with octagonal *bezel* inscribed with Lombardic letter A amidst sprigs. Triple fluted shoulders. Fifteenth century. Hoop D.: 22 (225).

2   Silver signet, the oval *bezel* with squirrel above a branch cracking nuts and *black letter* t. Found at Hereford. Fifteenth century (272).

3   Gold signet with a) round *bezel* engraved with trefoil, each petal inscribed with a letter, c m u, perhaps for the French C'EST MON URE or it is my destiny; b) view of wreathed hoop inscribed ESPOIRE DE MOI SANS FYNE, translating 'always pray for me'. Fifteenth century. Hoop D.: 21 (274).

The usual choice of those wishing to establish an individual mark of ownership but not entitled to bear arms was the personal cipher or initial. The owner of the ring with a 't' has combined his with a squirrel, admired for exemplifying the virtues of thrift and husbandry. Continually before the eyes, the request for prayers on the gold ring shows how the faith that built the cathedrals and sent pilgrims on their travels abroad was very much a feature of everyday life.

Fig. 2
Detail from margin of manuscript of jeweller's shop, fifteenth century, reproduced courtesy of the Bodleian Library, Ms Astor A24/II.

1   2

3a   3b

Plate 11

Ecclesiastical

1   The Thame reliquary ring. Paris, fourteenth century. The broad flat hoop is paved with five curved *table
cut* amethysts, with two more at each shoulder between
roundels. The large transverse oblong box *bezel* is set
with a large amethyst cross of Lorraine, with Lombardic
letters reserved in the upper and lower corners and
round the sides spelling out MEMANTO MEI DOMINE
(Remember me O Lord). The cover can be removed
showing a cavity for a relic, presumably a splinter from
the True Cross. The base and top plate were formerly
enamelled in colours with a leafy branch and on the
back there is a Crucifixion, with the Virgin and St.John
standing on either side of the cross. Made for an important prelate. Found with coins and rings in the Thame
Hoard in 1940. *Bezel* H.: 25; W.: 16. Hoop D.: 25 (AN
1940.228).

Fig. 3
Back of ring with engraving of Crucifixion and letters on sides.

40

1

Plate 12

Fifteenth- and early sixteenth-century Iconographic rings

1   Gold iconographic ring with a) triple *bezel* with Virgin and Child flanked by SS Helena and Barbara; b) view of shoulders with the Holy Trinity and St.John the Baptist. Hoop D.: 20 (265).

2   Gold iconographic ring a) with double *bezel* representing the Trinity and St.Barbara; b) view of inside with *black letter* inscription EN BON AN. Hoop D.: 17 (269).

3   Gold iconographic ring with St.George. Hoop D.: 18 (264).

4   Gold iconographic ring with double *bezel* representing the Virgin and Child with St.Christopher. Hoop D.: 21 (267).

The cult of patron saints is represented by this group known as 'iconographic' because they depict devotional images and saints, the most popular being as here, the Virgin and Child, the Trinity, and SS Christopher, Barbara, and Catherine. Used at weddings and given as New Year presents in England and Scotland from the late fourteenth century, the type did not survive the Reformation.

1a

1b

2b

2a

3

4

Plate 13

Magical rings set with toadstones and ass's hoof

1   Gold ring, the quatrefoil cusped *bezel* set with a toadstone. From the Thame Hoard, late fourteenth–fifteenth centuries. Hoop D.: 23 (AN 1940.225).

2   Silver ring with twin *bezels* each set with a toadstone for double power. Seventeenth century. Hoop D.: 23 (299).

3   Silver signet with unidentified shield of arms surmounted by letter L mounted on ass's hoof hoop. German, late sixteenth century. Hoop D.: 23 (248).

Wonderworking properties, such as the power to counteract epilepsy and dropsy were attributed to ass's hoof and toadstone (palatal tooth of the fossilised fish Lepidotus) respectively. In Scotland, according to Sir Walter Scott, they were believed efficacious well into the eighteenth century for Joanna Baillie told him that neighbours borrowed her mother's toadstone for the protection of their new born babies.

Fig. 4
Woodcut showing extraction of stone from the forehead of a toad. From Johannis de Cuba, *Ortis Sanitatis,* Strasbourg, 1483. Reproduced courtesy of the Bodleian Library, Ms. Douce 260.

1

2

3

Plate 14

Medieval and Renaissance love rings

1   Gold hoop of a) interlaced ribbons, engraved with sprigs and French *black letter* inscription MERCY, repeated five times; b) view of inside with heart and inscription MON AMOUR, fifteenth century. Hoop D.: 17 (277).

2   Gold ring, the *bezel* surmounted by a dog, symbolic of fidelity, winged shoulders. Sixteenth century. Hoop D.: 16 (111).

3   Gold ring, the revolving *bezel* set with a pearl. Similar rings are depicted in Italian paintings of the Mystic Marriage of St. Catherine. From Chalcis, fifteenth century. Hoop D.: 18 (F 376).

An essential part of the ritual of courtship and marriage, the ring in the Middle Ages intended for that purpose is inscribed with affectionate messages or posies (from poesies or little poems), and decorated with symbols such as the heart and the dog.

Fig. 5
A falconer gives a ring, set with a stone, to a lady who holds her pet squirrel close to her breast, with a dog symbolic of fidelity seated between them. From the Ormesby Psalter, *c*.1310–25. Reproduced courtesy of the Bodleian Library, Ms. Douce 366.

1a

1b

2

3

Plate 15

The Renaissance love and marriage ring

1   Silver ring, the round *bezel nielloed* with lovers face to face. Umbrian, fifteenth century. Hoop D.: 20 (69).

2   Silver and *niello* hoop with Italian inscription AMORE VOLE FE translating 'Love cannot exist without fidelity', as inscribed on the scroll in the print below. Umbrian, fifteenth century. Hoop D.: 18 (72).

3   Gold signet *fede* ring with a) oval *bezel* set with red jasper zodiacal *intaglio* of Leo beneath stars and crescent, a dolphin on the back; b) hoop terminating at base with pair of clasped hands. Gem second century A.D., ring sixteenth century. Hoop D.: 18 (92).

4   Gold *fede* ring, the *bezel* with two hands clasped in love and friendship emerging from cuffed sleeves. Sixteenth century. Hoop D.: 16 (95).

The theme of love is expressed by the posy and double portrait on the two *nielloed* silver rings from Umbria, and by two *'fede'* rings with hands clasped together in love and trust. This symbol of the pledging of vows which derives from the Roman *dextrarum iunctio* reappears in early medieval rings and continues in use with the Irish *Claddagh* ring today.

Fig. 6
Print of two lovers face to face, perhaps Lorenzo de Medici (1449–92) and Lucretia Donati each holding scrolls inscribed AMORE VOLE FE as in ring no.2 above, Cabinet des Estampes.

1

2

3a

3b

4

Plate 16

The Renaissance love and marriage ring continued

1   Gold *gimmel* ring, the double quatrefoil *bezel* set with four well matched rubies, petals chased and enamelled, twin hoops inscribed in Latin MEMENTO PRAE-TERIT ET FUTURI TEMPORIS STET translating 'Remember the past and that there is a future'. Sixteenth century. Hoop D.: 16 (90).

2   Gilt bronze traveller's locket ring, the a) oval *bezel* set with a *foiled crystal intaglio* with forget-me-nots date 1579, and VMN for VERGISS MEIN NICHT translating 'forget me not'; b) opening to show compass, numbers 1–12 incised round edge. Sixteenth century. Hoop D.: 23 (242).

Gimmel (from the Latin gemellus, for twin) rings with double hoops and *bezels* like two lovers side by side, being used for weddings, are usually inscribed with the words from the Gospel asserting the indissolubility of the marriage vows, or as here with a reminder of the limitations of earthly happiness. The forget-me-not motif was also adopted by lovers in England, with the letters FMN instead of the German abbreviation VMN. This example is more than a love token for the compass inside is useful for travellers, and the crystal *intaglio* can also be used as a seal.

Fig. 7
Detail of G.B.Moroni, The Mystic Marriage of St. Catherine, showing the Infant Jesus holding the ring for his marriage with the saint seated before him. Ashmolean Museum.

50

1

2a

2b

Plate 17

The Jewish marriage ring

1   Gold ring, gabled roof *bezel.* a) The wide hoop surmounted by steep pinnacled gabled roof, b) *bezel,* Hebrew inscription MAZAL TOV or Good Luck! Hoop D.: 18 (52).

2   Gold ring, the wide hoop with filigree and granulation scrolling vine between corded wire borders. Hoop D.: 18 (50).

3   Gold ring with a) wide hoop with massive corded wire borders enclosing filigree *bosses* alternating with leaves, surmounted by hinged imbricated blue roof *bezel;* b) *bezel* opened to Hebrew inscription MAZAL TOV, or Good Luck! Hoop D.: 19 (56).

4   Gold ring, the a) wide hoop with filigree *bosses* between pairs of quatrefoils within corded wire border; b) surmounted by a pearl canopy on Solomonic pillars over Hebrew inscription MAZAL TOV. This exceptional ring represents the canopy under which the bride and groom made their vows, as shown in fig.8 below. Hoop D.: 18 (55).

In use from the Middle Ages, Jewish wedding rings have a distinctive character represented by the types represented here which include wide and narrow hoops, those surmounted by a building or tiled roof and exceptionally, by the marriage canopy. Most, as here, are inscribed in Hebrew translating 'Good Luck'. Their place of origin remains unknown, for although traditionally ascribed to Venice where there was a large Jewish population, they are closer in style to the enamelled gold filigree work of Transylvanian goldsmiths.

Fig. 8
Woodcut of Jewish marriage in Venice, 1601. Reproduced courtesy of the Bodleian Library.

1a

1b

טוב

2

3a

3b

4a

4b

Plate 18

The Renaissance signet

1   Gold signet with *foiled crystal intaglio* with an *achievement* perhaps of the Stoke family, initials TS; view of shoulders with *strap, volutes and bosses.* English, late sixteenth century. Hoop D.: 24 (286).

2   Silver signet with round *bezel* engraved with shield of arms surmounted by a cross, flanked by letters TO, perhaps that of the family of Alberighi. Italian, sixteenth century. Hoop D.: 19 (190).

3   Gold signet with oval *bezel* engraved with initials SH linked by Bowen knot. Hoop D.: 29 (282).

4   Gold signet with oval *bezel* engraved with merchant's mark and letters DF. Hoop D.: 20 (290).

Made for daily use, Renaissance signets are therefore of solid and simple design, the exception being the more decorative *foiled crystal intaglio* engraved with a coat of arms with colours painted on foil beneath. An important non- armorial type is the 'merchant' or trade mark proving ownership of goods and which was therefore painted on shop fronts, warehouses and merchandise.

Fig. 9
Illustration of bale of goods stamped with merchant's mark from window in Tournai Cathedral.

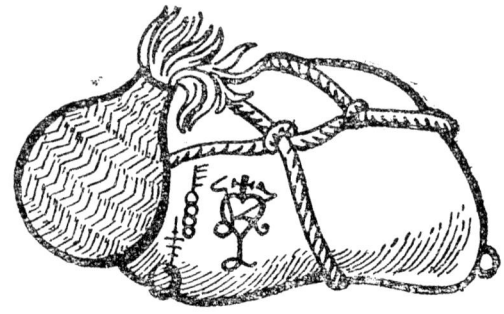

1

2

3

4

Plate 19

The Renaissance decorative gem set ring

1   Gold ring with quatrefoil *bezel* set with a *table cut* ruby, cusped shoulders. Hoop D.: 18 (160).

2   Gold ring with quatrefoil *bezel*: set with a *cabochon* sapphire, petals subdivided and chased with double crescents and formal ornament, shoulders with scrolls and *strapwork*, formerly enamelled. Hoop D.: 18 (114).

3   Gold ring with oblong box *bezel* set with a *table cut* diamond, on cushion, sides enamelled with crescents, cast symmetrical *strapwork* on the shoulders, enamelled green, white and black. Hoop D.: 19 (135).

4   Gold ring with octagonal *bezel* set with *cabochon* ruby, sides chased with crescents on gadrooned base: winged shoulders. Hoop D.: 18 (115).

Although *cabochon* stones are still used in sixteenth-century rings, the progress in faceting is illustrated by the *table cut* diamond and ruby. The standard quatrefoil *bezel* may be left plain but more usually the petals are enriched by chasing and enamelling. Equally distinctive are the winged, raised and pierced shoulders ornamented with *strap, bosses* and quatrefoils which are not subordinate to the setting but play an equal role in the design.

Fig. 10
Designs for gem set rings by Etienne Delaune, Ashmolean Museum.

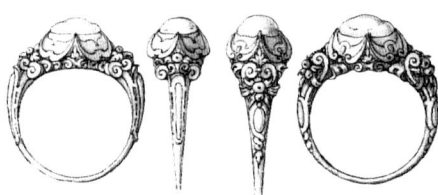

1

2   3

4

Plate 20

Death in Renaissance and later rings

1   Gold hexagonal *bezel* with incurved sides with skull enamelled within inscription BEHOLD THE EN. English, sixteenth century. Hoop D.: 19 (278).

2   Gold ring with black and white skull resting on cross bones, diamonds set in bones, in eye sockets, nose and in groups of three at top, base and sides of skull. Back enamelled with white cross bones between crowns on black ground. Seventeenth century. Hoop D.: 18 (191).

3   Gold and enamel ring with janiform *bezel* representing a) a young woman, blonde and radiant with youth, with b) skull behind, heads crowned with a diamond. Shoulders with harlequin stones and with bay leaves flanking the skull, musical instruments, the woman's head, enamelled green, white and black. Seventeenth century. Hoop D.: 19 (201).

4   Gold ring with a) square box *bezel* set with an amethyst fluted sides filled with black enamel dotted with white; b) flanked by skull and cross bones at the shoulders. Seventeenth century. Hoop D.: 19 (148).

Mortality rates were high in the sixteenth and seventeenth centuries, due to war, plague and famine. It is in this atmosphere that rings with Memento Mori symbols acknowledged the brevity and vanities of life, and the need to prepare for death by contemplating coffins, skulls, hour glasses, and the grave digger's pick and shovel.

Fig. 11
Pierre Woeriot, *Livre d'Aneaux* (Lyon 1561) design for memento mori ring.

58

1

2

3a

3b

4a

4b

Plate 21

Decorative seventeenth-century styles

1   Gold solitaire ring, the a) inverted pyramidal *bezel* set with table diamond held in eagle's claws; b) hoop and shoulders enamelled black. Hoop D.: 18 (137).

2   Gold seven stone cluster ring, the wide *bezel* with sides enamelled black and white set with a *table cut* diamond in lozenge setting, flanked by three smaller diamonds. Hoop D.: 18 (154).

3   Gold cluster ring, the round *bezel* set with rubies and turquoises centred on a *table cut* diamond. Hoop D.: 19 (159).

4   Gold ring, the square *bezel* set with a ruby (?) sides enamelled white with black details; b) back with Sacred Monogram, IHS, the abbreviated name of Christ, three nails and cross. Hoop D.: 19 (206).

Around 1600 a new chapter opens in the history of jewellery which is henceforward concerned primarily with the display of stones. These are now the focus of ring design, whether solitaires or in clusters, and the shoulders and hoop are now subordinate to the *bezel*. Since large gems were rare and expensive, jewellers had to make do with the smaller specimens, grouping them into attractive patterns of which the seven stone cluster was the most popular.

Fig. 12
Detail (hand only) Johannes Cornelisz. Verspronck (1597–1662) Portrait of a Lady *c.*1642, showing diamond solitaire similar to 1 above. (Private collection and on loan to the Ashmolean Museum).

1a

1b

2

3

4a

4b

Plate 22

Seventeenth-century signets

1   Gold signet, the octagonal *bezel* set with chalcedony engraved with an unidentified marriage *achievement*, sides and shoulders with *blackwork* ornament. German. Hoop D.: 16 (240).

2   Gold signet, the octagonal *bezel* set with a *foiled crystal intaglio* engraved with a shield of arms and the letters EHZ and PGZW, blackwork sides of *bezel* and shoulders, each with table diamond, hoop shaped to thumb. Hoop D.: 23 (241).

3   Gold signet, the oval *bezel* with unidentified crest, initials RB at back with London hallmark and mark of Isaac Davenport, 1689–90. Hoop D.: 16 (287).

4   Gold signet, the octagonal *bezel* engraved with an eagle with two heads, hallmark for York 1664. Hoop D.: 21 (288).

5   Gold ring with swivel *bezel* one side with white skull and black inscription MEMENTO MORI; b) the other side with the shield of arms of Harman of Suffolk. Hoop D.: 19 (280).

The transition from the bright enamels of the sixteenth century to seventeenth century sobriety begins with 'blackwork' ornament illustrated here, in use *c.*1585–1620. Thereafter signet rings become rarer, eclipsed by the fashion for wearing the seal in an ornamental mount designed to hang from a chain beside the watch.

1

2

3

4

5a

5b

Plate 23

Seventeenth-century love rings

1   Gold and enamel *gimmel* ring, a) the *bezel* formed of two white hands clasped, set with a *cabochon* ruby, flanked by shoulders with white and ruby hearts applied; b) twin hoops inscribed in Roman capitals WAS GOT ZU SAMEN FIGET DAS SOL DER MENSCH NIT SCHAIDEN, translating 'What God has joined together let no man put asunder' (St.Mark, X, v.9). Hoop D.: 17 (199).

2   Gold ring, with eagle's claws gripping the star shaped *bezel* set with a point cut and four triangular diamonds, blackwork shoulders, two clasped hands at the base of the hoop. Hoop D.: 17 (198).

3   Gold ring, the heart shaped *bezel* set with a sapphire within a ruby border. Hoop D.: 19 (162).

4   Gold ring inscribed with the posy PROVIDENCE DIVINE HATH MADE THEE MINE. Hoop D.: 19 (332).

5   Gold ring inscribed with posy WHOE FEARES THE LORD ARE BLEST WEE SEE /SUCH THOU AND I GOD GRANT MAY BE. Hoop D.: 17 (338).

Although *gimmel*, heart and *fede* rings continue in use for love and marriage during the seventeenth century they are greatly outnumbered by plain gold bands inscribed with posies such as these acknowledging and asking for God's blessing. It was not until the Wedding Rings Act of 1855 which made hallmarking compulsory, taking up the space needed for the posies, that these give way to narrow hoops bearing nothing more than the initials of the bride and groom and the date of the marriage.

Fig. 13
G.Withers, *Collection of Emblems* (1635) engraving of heart burning with love held by clasped hands of two lovers.

1a

1b

2

3

4

5

Plate 24

Memorial rings

1 Gold ring surmounted by a crown held by two angels, the round *bezel* with indented border set with a rose cut crystal over monogram TS in gold thread: black and white foliate shoulders. Late seventeenth century. Hoop D.: 18 (372).

2 Gold hoop ring, enamelled black with hour glass and grave digger's pick and shovel inscribed within IS OBT 24 JUNE 1713 AET 60. Hoop D.: 15 (386).

3 Gold and black enamel a) coffin shaped *bezel* with skull and crowned monogram above plaited hair inside covered by glass; b) the hoop inscribed outside ANNA REGINA PIA FELIX, the inside NAT 6 FEB 1664 IN AUG 8 MAR(CH) 1701 OBT 1 AUG (T) l714. English, early eighteenth century. Hoop D.: 15 (373).
The death of Queen Anne, the last of the Stuart dynasty, led to the succession of the Hanoverian king George I whose descendants have continued to occupy the British throne.

4 Gold memorial ring, a) the coffin shaped *bezel* enclosing an urn enamelled white and set with diamonds bordered by amethysts and b) with cavity for hair. White hoop inscribed AB OB MAY 19 1755: IF I FORGET THEE. Hoop D.: 19 (375).

In the course of the seventeenth century memento mori rings were superseded by rings commemorating a deceased individual whose initials were executed in gold thread, and then by inscriptions on a black hoop giving the name and date of death. The use of white instead of black enamel indicates that the deceased was unmarried.

66

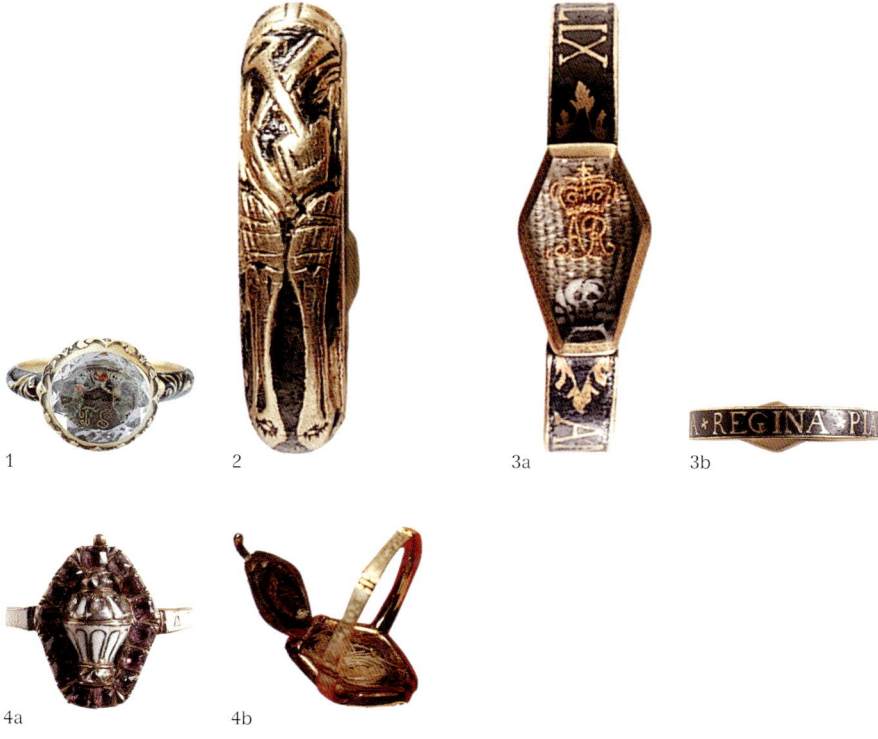

1

2

3a

3b

4a

4b

Plate 25

Rococo style *'giardinetti'* or decorative rings

1   Gold and silver ring, the openwork flower *bezel* set with rose and *table cut* diamonds, and *table cut* rubies. Stylised leaf hoop. Hoop D.: 17 (175).

2   Gold and silver ring, the openwork five petalled flower *bezel* set with garnets and rose cut diamonds. Stylised leaf hoop. Hoop D.: 17 (177).

3   Gold and silver ring, the openwork flower *bezel* set with diamond sparks, rubies and a topaz. Stylised leaf hoop. Hoop D.: 17 (176).

4   Gold and silver ring, the openwork *bezel* formed as a diamond vase with ruby emerald and diamond flowers. *Reeded* hoop. Hoop D.: 18 (181).

5   Gold and diamond ring, the openwork *bezel* in the form of a diamond and ruby spray of three petalled flowers tied with a ribbon. Stylised leaf hoop. Hoop D.: 15 (179).

6   Gold and silver ring, the openwork *bezel* forming a spray of ruby and diamond flowers. Stylised leaf hoop. Hoop D.: 18 (180).

Rings of coloured stones set in gold with diamonds in silver in asymmetrical openwork sprays of flowers or 'little gardens' tied with ribbons or in vases are the jewelled counterparts of those decorating contemporary textiles and ceramics. They illustrate rococo taste for light and delicate designs.

Fig. 14
Designs for *giardinetti* rings by Christian Taute, *c*.1750. Victoria and Albert Museum.

68

1

2

3

4

5

6

Plate 26

Rococo style 'alliance' or love and marriage rings

1   Gold and silver ring, the *bezel* set with a ruby simulating two hearts overlapping, tied with a golden ribbon, and aflame with diamond sparks. Rose diamond shoulders. Hoop D.: 15 (171).

2   Gold and silver ring, the *bezel* with twin hearts, respectively set with a rose cut diamond and a *table cut* ruby, within diamond borders and surmounted by a diamond and ruby coronet. Hoop D.: 18 (169).

3   Gold and silver ring, the *bezel* with two hearts, set with a flat rose cut diamond and a *table cut* ruby respectively, surmounted by a five pointed diamond coronet, with two diamonds below. Openwork shoulders, one filled with a ruby, the other with a diamond. Hoop D.: 17 (173).

4   Gold and silver ring, the *bezel* set with twin hearts, set with a ruby and a diamond respectively and surmounted by a diamond coronet, shoulders set respectively with a ruby and a diamond. Hoop D.: 17 (172).

5   Gold and silver ring with openwork *bezel* of twin interlaced ribbon ruby and diamond hearts. Flowers and leaves at the shoulders. Hoop D.: 20 (174).

The motif of the heart, united with another, crowned, burning or tied with a knot in a light, openwork design was used for eighteenth-century 'alliance' or wedding rings. The twin hearts are sometimes differentiated by being respectively set with a ruby and a diamond.

1

2

3

4

5

Plate 27

The neoclassical ring

1   Gold ring, the a) oval *bezel* set with an 'eye' sardonyx, framed within a blue and white enamelled border. Open at the back; b) Hoop expanding to faceted shoulders edged with husks enamelled blue and white. Hoop D.: 20 (144).

2   Gold ring with oval *bezel* set with lapis lazuli on which is applied a chased gold figure of Diana extinguishing the torch of daylight called 'of the Mountains' a replica of the gem signed APOLLONIDES, from the Farnese collection in Naples. Hoop D.: 18 (143).

The revival of classical principles in art of the 1770s is illustrated by these severe, symmetrical designs, both large enough to cover most of the finger. The replica of the famous Diana gem on the finger established the owner as a person of taste and learning, and the perfect 'eye' sardonyx indicated his appreciation of the beauties of nature.

Fig. 15
Designs for neoclassical rings with large octagonal *bezels*. Reproduced courtesy of the Victoria and Albert Museum.

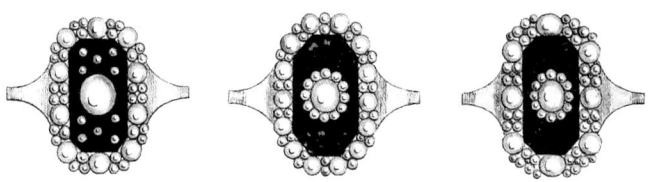

1a

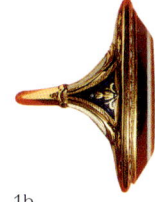

1b

2

Plate 28

Death and sentiment

1   Gold ring, the marquise *bezel* containing a lock of white hair tied with a gold ribbon on blue ground outlined in white and beaded gold border within a seed pearl frame *c.*1770. Hoop D.: 19 (379).

2   Gold ring, the marquise *bezel* with glass over plaited hair enclosing ivory plaque with shield bearing initials AAD flanked by palm branches and surmounted by swags, the back inscribed AAD to ED. English, *c.*1770. Hoop D.: 19 (378).

These neat, pointed oval, or marquise rings enclosing the hair of a beloved individual living or dead were worn by those who preferred to demonstrate sentiment rather than wealth. They can be linked with the success of the novel, by J.J.Rousseau, *La Nouvelle Héloïse* (1761) depicting the ideal society which results when love and virtue are united against the simple background of nature away from the artificial world of court life.

Fig. 16
Trade card of Hill, a London jeweller, advertising rings of sentiment, 1791. Copyright The British Museum.

74

1

2

Plate 29

Rings associated with illustrious people and political
events: Italy

1   Coral ring, a) the *bezel* with portrait of Urban
VIII; b) flanked at shoulders by standing figures of SS
Peter and Paul each holding a book, and attributes, keys
and sword respectively. Matteo Barberini, Pope 1624–
1644. Hoop D.: 16 (166).

2   Gold ring, enamelled black a) the oval locket *bezel*
bearing diamond cipher crowned VE; b) miniature inside, flanked by letter V at shoulders. Victor Emmanuel
II, King of Italy (1820–1878): the first king of a united
Italy who carried his countrymen from despondency to
triumph. Hoop D.: 18 (141).

From antiquity onwards portrait rings have been distributed during
their lifetime by those in positions of spiritual or temporal power as
marks of favour to those loyal to them. Urban VIII, patron of G.L.
Bernini who did much to embellish the city of Rome may have given
the coral cameo ring to an important pilgrim. Similarly their memo-
ry was honoured by memorial rings such as that commemorating
Victor Emmanuel II, who had a large patriotic following.

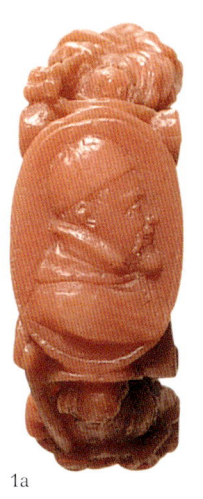

1a   1b

2a   2b

Plate 30

Illustrious people and political events: Great Britain

1   Gold ring with oval *bezel* enclosing miniature of
Charles I (1600–1649) against a celestial blue ground.
Hoop D.: 17 (293).
A ring worn by a Jacobite. demonstrating loyalty to the
House of Stuart in exile.

2   Gold ring with oval *bezel* set with a crystal over
miniature of the Old Pretender James Francis Edward
Stuart, the Chevalier of Saint-George also known to his
followers as James III (1688–1766), miniature of his wife,
Clementina Sobieska, at the back. The ring was removed
from the finger of their younger son, Cardinal York
(1725–1807) on his death bed when the male line of the
Royal House of Stuart became extinct. Hoop D.: 17 (392).

3   Gold ring the oval *bezel* set with a cairngorm and
flanked by Prince of Wales feathers, initials CPR, Irish
harp at back.
Presented by Prince Charles Edward during the 1745
campaign. Hoop D.: 21·5 (AN loan 514).

4   Gold ring, the oval *bezel* set with a miniature of
George Handel (1685–1759). Hoop D.: 17 (380).

5   Gold ring, the oval *bezel* set with moss agate landscape. Hoop D.: 18 (366).
This ring belonged to the master of English landscape
painting Thomas Gainsborough, (1727–1788) whose
descendant, Mrs Poole, presented it to the Ashmolean
Museum.

1

2

3

4

5

Glossary

Achievement: representing all the armorial devices to which a bearer of arms is entitled.
Bezel: the part of the ring which sits on the top of the finger, set with a gem or bearing a device flanked by the shoulders which merge with the round hoop.
Black letter: angular script of the Gothic period.
Black work: type of enamelling in use from 1590–1620 with broken scroll ornament silhouetted against a black or white enamel ground.
Boss: protuberance or knob.
Cabochon: the stone in its original domed form, polished but not faceted, the back flat.
Claddagh: the wives of fishermen in Claddagh of Galway traditionally wear rings with clasped hands on the *bezel*. They are handed down as heirlooms from mother to daughter.
Dextrarum iunctio: Latin translating the joining of right hands, the Roman name for motif of clasped hands used on rings as token of agreement to terms of a contract and subsequently adopted as a symbol of love and marriage.
Faience: a vitreous paste which has a beautiful blue green glaze when fired.

Fede: Italian translating trust, for the clasped hands motif used for love and marriage rings.
Foiled crystal intaglio: technique used for signet rings by which the colours of the coat of arms are painted on foil and then covered by a rock crystal *intaglio* from which an impression can be taken for seals, and which protects the colours from fading.
Giardinetti: Italian translating 'little gardens' known in English as flower pot rings because of the arrangements of flowers on the *bezels*. They date from the middle to the third quarter of the eighteenth century.
Gimmel: from the Latin 'gemellus', meaning a ring with twin hoops and *bezels*, used for marriage on account of the symbolism.
Intaglio: The engraving technique by which the device is incised below the surface of the stone so that an impression can be taken from it for sealing.
Keeled: with a ridge in the centre.
Niello: Ornament obtained by the fusion of a black sulphurous composition with silver.
Strap: bands, derived from narrow strips of leather, folded and interlaced.
Table cut: the simplest form of faceting a stone flat by removing the top point or dome.
Volute: spiral form of classical origin.

Bibliography

Extensive bibliographies can be found in:

B.Chadour, *Ringe der Alice und Louis Koch Sammlung* (Leeds 1994) II, pp 637–654.
D.Scarisbrick, *Rings, Symbols of Love,*

Power and Affection (London 1993), pp 219–220.
G.Taylor and D.Scarisbrick, *Finger Rings from Ancient Egypt to the Present Day* (Oxford 1978).

Accession numbers and measurements

The captions to each plate include the accession numbers, which identify each individual ring within the Museum's collections. The rings in Part 1 are all from the Department of Antiquities, bearing the prefix AN. The rings in Part 2 are, in the main, from the Department of Western Art from the collection bequeathed to the Museum by C.D.E.Fortnum in 1899. The one, two or three digit numbers in brackets after each entry are the Gallery reference numbers; those prefixed by the letter F are the Fortnum collection references. The measurements of the hoops – and in the case of most of the antique rings – of the *bezels*, are given in millimetres, immediately preceding the accession number.